"Sue Westwind's *Man Dies, Leaves Widow on Earth* is a poignant testament to the human experience, expressed through the delicate artistry of poetry. With a voice that resonates profoundly, Westwind captures the essence of life's most profound moments—death, survival, grief, and resilience. In this remarkable cycle of poems, Westwind demonstrates a lyrical power that transcends the page, drawing readers into narratives that feel intimately personal yet universally relatable. Her ability to weave together the threads of sorrow and hope, tragedy and triumph, is nothing short of mesmerizing.

"What sets Westwind apart as a poet is her unwavering honesty. She confronts the complexities of grief with a fearless gaze, inviting readers to accompany her on a journey through the depths of sorrow and the heights of joy. She unveils the raw emotions that pulse beneath the surface of existence, leaving an indelible mark on the soul. So, immerse yourself in the luminous world of Sue Westwind's poetry. You will emerge transformed, touched by the profound beauty of her words and the depth of her insight. This is poetry that lingers, that resonates long after the final page is turned."

— DORA CARPENTER, author of *Grief Talk Revolution* and *From Grief to Gratitude*

Man Dies,
Leaves Widow on Earth

SAY YES QUICKLY BOOKS

7715 East Highland Avenue

Scottsdale, Arizona 85251 USA

Copyright © 2024 by Sue Westwind.

All rights reserved.

No portion of this book may be reproduced in any form without written permission from the publisher or author, except as permitted by U.S. copyright law.

Cover photograph by Austin Chan / Unsplash

ISBN: 979-8-9898660-8-3

First print edition.

SUE WESTWIND

Man Dies,
Leaves Widow on Earth

A Cycle of Poems on
Intimacy, Nature & Grief

SAY YES QUICKLY BOOKS

for Nora Beth, Noelle, Nylah, and Knox

By these songs may you glimpse the great-uncle you never knew.
May the sorrows you meet be held with a compassionate heart.

Contents

PART I: The Grief Season 1

Where Are You? 3

The Absence of Animal 7

Riverdusk on the Kaw 11

The Monastic Side of It 15

Here Come the Holidays 19

Easter Snow Day 23

Numbers Game 25

PART II: Season's Helpers 29

Why the Grieving Read 31

He Touched It 33

Aloft and At Rest 37

The Grief Group 39

Sister Widow 43

Left on Earth 45

PART III: Post-Season 49

The Bereaved Dead	51
The Song Cycles Around	53
Yet Another Burst	57
I Can Tell	61
Grief-Light for the Earth	65
Remedy	69
About the Author	73

PART I: The Grief Season

Where Are You?

Trains vanquish this soil, dark crumble

of river bottom—a wealth long drained

of value, paved and mute.

The loss of this ground's glory

was a death I missed—unlike yours,

when the layered heft of intimacy

we call marriage ended within earshot

of trains hollering but never knowing:

us.

Neighbors fight over whether to revile

the engines' timed screams or relish them

as this hood's badge of honor.

You and I lost our home far from

this quibble, moved here among these

plain houses as we were stroke-weary

and wondering: how long until your brain

traveled to its last clotted event—

the one where you left me on Earth?

One train competed with the wail of

your last ambulance pulling to the curb.

Engines huff blessedly softer when

winter closes the house, but trains

matter much less now because

you're not in your chair beside me,

feet up and grumbling about the noise,

telling me the crew is full of spite as

they detonate sound into innocent streets.

Today trains clack about how life

goes on, how speed is of the essence.

The surrounding air they take by force

isn't of your world,

a world we call Next or Other,

an air I imagine rarified yet specific,

not even a vapor or weight. Energy?

No one is sure.

I fall to common preoccupations

of the widow, a need to know

if her mate made it soul intact

to some place grand. Or safe.

Sleeping through the clatter

I collect dreams:

you running through a wooded trail

in freedom and glee, smiling

at the certainty: there's no chance

of cardiovascular mishap now.

I wake to the pull of the cemetery,

where once a pair of bald eagles

flew over your grave—

that was me with upturned face

marking their flight, mind suspended

in the slosh of time, looking for signs.

But today, lost in meditation,

burnished light on my eyelids

where shapes whirled not exactly

like birds, not exactly like anything—

was it you?

Do you still love me?

Are you able to help?

These are the questions

no trains can drown out,

all that's left when missing you

is classified, complex work

to be done whenever it gets done,

a snail's-pace pilgrimage into grief

made artful by each moment

that I linger, curious and raw, waiting

for the ebb of an obsession

more riveting in some ways

than was the torrent of falling in love.

The Absence of Animal

The bed's no longer a refuge

where thoughts and plans

are conquered,

but a cold envelope

to slide into,

begrudged and afraid.

I sleep on your side.

Even though you stopped

touching me long before the end—

sitting across the divide

that only cable news bridged—

there was that tangible orbit

that holds couples in place when years

match the day-in to the day-out.

The animal nudge and muster of love.

Without it, patched by unspoken

words that mend the breaches

born of anger and regret

I float, hardly physical, evaporating.

What's left? Mind and memory,

not always kind. Household altars

can't tug the wondering widow

back into her flesh.

Yet these mantles of memory

keep the awful image at bay:

what becomes of your body.

Cold from the minute Death handled you

in its waxen way, then crushed under the

weight of winter's most frozen earth,

no longer the you that smiles,

photogenic husband, from pictures

in every room. Why stare at these

framed shrines when you'll never wear

that face again? The mate-animal,

man-animal, father-animal is gone.

Trapped here and too tired to wake,

grown dull to stuff and circumstance,

I try to find the default position

where life reveals its winning card.

Pleasure.

That thing for other people to sample or stew.

Riverdusk on the Kaw

Why do I exalt the dim of day

next to this silver ribbon

where ice hunks float like

pieces of ragged trash?

One look upriver shows

the twinkle of downtown shifting

from commerce to juke joint,

while a squawking V of geese

splits overhead, getting in

the last word before sunset's fire.

Alone as I can be,

the structure of each day

mangled past reason,

my heart races for this:

to be outdoors when light-points

on houses and apartments appear,

mica bits of shine that wink

as downstream eases itself

into a land of shades. I praise

the human urge for home

at this hour, be it a hive

or hoard of heavy silence—

an enclosure that receives.

Riverdusk watches over the rites

of settling in. Attempts the erasure

of hurts and gains. Ignored by most,

it knows only what's good for them.

But if I gorge on the scene too long,

I'll walk to my four walls in darkness.

It's not the fear of harm that troubles—

not on these carefully known streets.

Glancing toward windows,

most not yet curtained but soft like

eyes onto lives where screens festoon,

where knickknacks play on shelves,

the angles of sink, bedpost, sofa back—

where are the people?

Not meant to be seen.

I can't check on them

to make sure they hear

how Death steps closer

minute by ignored minute,

the herald who calls them

to consider the water's meander,

to love without guarantee

of identical heartbeats in return,

to find one of many hallelujahs

and sing it full-throated on their knees

in praise of how all things must end—

as riverdusk unhands them into night.

The Monastic Side of It

For hours I drink silence

and only in the hallway

note pain. Why is it that

in corridors the shedding

of weeks reveals the question:

what now?

Now is too large

for this mundane passage,

a tunnel emptying into

rooms that gape and hold

the sobs close.

Though I speak out loud

and often

in all rooms

to no one,

I can't fathom an answer

to what I fear are prods

from you—

to trip me up? Or offer

a friendly push?

If you told me to live in a way

that mimicked my mind

before your leaving,

I would do my best.

But who knows that I'm not

thriving as monks do in their

quiet caverns, the prayer in me

circumventing familiar gods

and put to Time itself:

please oust the uninvited guest

—*Loneliness*—who only relents

with distraction, and never in

these halls where love meets

its gruesome, holy match,

the grief that strips all hope trying

to imagine a story that doesn't

end badly like this one.

Here Come the Holidays

I.

Man dies ten days before Thanksgiving.
Relatives don't invite widow and children
to their homes. "We thought you
wouldn't want to drive that far!"
(Four hours. She's done it before.)
"It never occurred to us!" they crow,
as if this is reason enough.
The underlying rift is simple:
widow and brood do not meet
their religious criteria. And we have
a tendency to speak our minds
about anything, including the dead.

II.

Christmas Day. She sets the table

with a place for him, photos

of the smile he could always manage

despite the currency of stress—

she wonders if he will come

from the spirit world to sit nearby.

Daughters seem to understand.

It's only the three of us, on overdrive

to make brave and onward-lauding

sounds about how we have healed.

III.

The next year. We are up for grabs.

The biggest dread, confirmed,

is that outlier family, if even predisposed

to see us, will never mention

the dead man's name. Not once.

Thinking to prevent our sorrow, possibly

holding their own world together.

The show must go on,

an apex where feast and giving prevail.

Into this siege of evergreen cheer

I carry a burden of longing for one

ceremonial observance of truth and tears,

a meditation on impermanence

in honor of the darkest night before

the rise of that lustrous rim,

the always-returning Solstice sun.

Easter Snow Day

As the year spun safely past new

and started to think about Spring,

I walked back from numb by way

of eggs, steeped in scenes:

how you sat solemn every year, dipping

the boiled spheres into unnatural colors,

only to see them emerge pale

as the contents of a robin's nest.

You weren't one for stickers and tags

but savored the patience of lowering

half an orb to one shade, flip a deft

reverse to dunk a different hue.

Then it was over: someone else could

hide and hunt and even eat the things.

This year the daughters rushed from brunch

to parties, grateful not to sit with missing you.

At the cemetery my solitary car nosed

to the edge of burial woods and I took in

the improvements: the path is graveled now,

limestone posts like ancient menhir

mark the area for fresh graves. Who thought

that a freezing Easter would drive me to you:

weeping without blame shooting in

terse ricochet, free to acknowledge again

the abyss your absence makes.

No longer hard-boiled in my anger and guilt,

my yolk a little green with envy over

where you've gone, my shell impenetrable.

The sky cried white as a hen's pearly gift this Easter

and I cracked open, pelted by memories

of your fierce attachments to special days and rituals,

when the man could honor the boy within.

Numbers Game

(KSZ, June 12, 1956 - November 12, 2017)

Numerology rose in ancient lands

so fast that the only address for

its birthplace is "unknown."

For the love of mathematics,

high priests and priestesses

worked the cipher of one's name

and date of arrival on earth

into a map of the soul.

Why did you choose 12?

The Gnostics called it the number

of completion. Myth and scripture

pulse with twelves. Twelve apostles.

Twelve knights of the Round Table.

Twelve gates and twelve foundations

at Jerusalem. The twelve Nidanas

of the Buddha way, the sun blazing

twelvefold through the Brahmapurana.

If only I could tie those grand vistas

to your life.

You worked. You collected goods.

This is all there is? I used to ask.

You closed the door on what you wanted

most: intimacy, Nature,

long moments with animal companions,

and peace.

Rest now on this your birthday,

I've brought flowers to your grave,

what we do to smooth the macabre.

Besides, the Summer is too new

and manhandles us with heat and torpor.

This day used to side with Spring.

Given your love of timepieces,

the entry and exit number fits:

it wrangles the hours and months

into completion, wraps up tasks

before moving on. In death, take twelve.

Travel the zodiac, savor the dozen notes

before the octave, be no longer Hercules

with his twelve labors.

You have met the number you need.

PART II: Season's Helpers

Why the Grieving Read

To stop dreading the world with its foreign aplomb,

to stop filtering all contact through the mammoth

fact of the loss, the loss, the loss.

Flinching at little sounds—a ghost visit, a sign?

Wrestling with scenes of the final asunder:

illness, accident, aging into the Big Forget,

or stroke—a sharp parting on an ordinary day.

How long to stop resenting a bevy of new tasks?

How long the crying that slits the chest or puts a spike

to eyes already riven to the point of vision impaired—

salt-streams that pierce the dam,

falling to triggers that pepper the day. In public, too.

When do you no longer talk to the lost one

in tongues of regret? What about the cemetery—
staying too long, or hating yourself for not going?
Getting his mail, wrapping up his accounts.
Wipe out his Facebook page?

How long it takes can't be solved by dictum,
anniversaries, or the advent of the new.
It takes as long as a human needs,
say the wisdom-keepers who write books
where the stricken search and mourn along.

So, heed their printed words, for they know.
They are our predecessors, unsung pilgrims
on the road to transformation, who stayed
and built temple-houses, planted gardens
and never strung fence to keep others out—

books given birth as the sense of motion quelled,
once Death became a teacher and an ally.
The grief writers reach with satchels of truth.
Unpack the bounty in your solitary cell.

He Touched It

Now, I am a woman who looks out

at things as if from another country

or from prison, where no messages

pass without inspection.

My canine friend rests while

I need a moment with the river,

where a metal swing rocks like home.

A man with dogs on leash

appears ahead and avidly regards

the water, his presence vigorous

even at a distance.

This is what I'd waited for:

someone cut loose from his job

his money and his house,

old enough to know things

but still feel things,

bald but still *alive*.

This had to exist: a force who

chooses to live in his body,

shirt a bit artsy,

shorts that reveal outdoor legs,

an apparition emerging from

the heart of the woods to here.

As if some spirit knew

I was longing for such a vision

the man bounces with his pooches

over to the looming statue

of a woman and her mate joined

back-to-back, fused in stone,

then places a hand on the surface

just below where her breasts

attach like halves of coconuts,

symmetrical but separate,

making me see them.

I look away too late as he whirls: "Hi!"

My echo is meek and the wind

slaps it away like a bug.

I let him go, how could I hold him?

Left with a pair of desires,

unseemly and forward,

improbable from the start:

to stand inside the space

the air made around him,

to place my hand on the stone

where his hand lingered,

stealing an essence my fingers

could hold all night.

Aloft and At Rest

Your Highness of treetops,

gleaming white head and tail,

have you come to allow us

passage beneath your perch?

Though we know this river

supports you and you know

we are drawn to its curvature,

sightings of you aloft and at rest

are rare. I see you scud the water

then land, tolerant above strollers,

a bicyclist, a man blocking birdsong

with headphones. May I look?

I've stopped such a respectful distance,

sending you my heart.

I think you are my husband, dark-bodied bird,

his spirit hitching a ride.

For he had ties to you. When you

winged across his path, the white cap

you wear taught him truths below words.

I had a silhouette of your kind etched

onto the stone where his body lies now

although he flies elsewhere.

Your massive head swivels,

one cornea the color of sun spies down.

You look away, then back to me,

nervous, ruffling.

Then you fly, pointedly, and I weigh

whether I'm unworthy or a trespasser

who got too close to resplendence

never meant to be pinned to the eye,

wildness never fashioned to palliate grief.

The Grief Group

When we broke up with each other

the timing was spontaneous:

stragglers whose visits slowed

with grace became the rule.

One by one we bowed out due to

the turn of a better tide.

Each left to applause and assent,

knowing they pushed those left

that much closer to the finish line.

But it should be remembered

how it all began:

a funeral home's largesse giving us

the skillful ferrywoman as our guide

pointing out the sights on the banks

of the River Lethe while holding us

back from jumping in to search for

the beloved, drowning.

We spoke the unspeakables:

about the slowing down of time,

the darkness no one else could see,

flashbacks not ripe for memories,

and the emptied house—shunned

by some but to others a haven

where the dead sat mute at the table,

tugged ever so slightly at the bed sheets,

or told the dogs of their presence.

Loosened from curriculum,

the group still gathered but in daylight,

places that bustled with noise

and commerce—as if being tossed

among normal people didn't grate.

Or was it that they needed to see us?

It was hard to crack the great prohibition

that we ourselves had once decried,

where small-talk and reports of busy doings

prevailed until we reached the subsurface,

sitting together stumped:

how to haul our ragged souls

through another day?

Bit by wrestled bit these stories

heartfully changed until

there was nothing left to say.

Sail on, my friends, mind your dreams

and know how legibly you are etched

as my once-so-necessary anchors,

when together we kept faith in the repair

of holes made by missing persons.

I don't think I could ever forget how

strongly you loved and suffered for love.

How gathering like the hunkered down

while a hurricane rages

was what kept us safe—

how we went looking, one by one,

for lives to live again, rebirthed by

each other and the scent of the world,

at last on a mission to bloom.

Sister Widow

She was the oracle consulted for a map,

she, a decade down the grief trail.

When she spoke I believed: she had lived through

what only battered around my periphery

like black holes designing the future.

A whole room in her home devoted to Frida Kahlo—

the sugar skulls, the bright palette, the bed waiting

for sleepers to contact feisty-sad Frida in dreams.

We watched a one-woman play depicting the great artist

so churned into her grief we forgot our own

in theatre rows of darkness, not knowing what to make

of a woman taming terror into *colores* and *formas*

as if pulled from the font of her broken womb.

Now my sister widow professes that only love will save her,

her oracular powers subsumed to online dating,

engaged with great weariness and the wisdom to sift quickly

through the hopeful faces. She nests with death by

giving away her possessions, sharing skills for a fine cabernet,

while standing at the fork on the trail:

either lunge into fierce self-care that heals her body into

a beacon signaling The One, or bow to the final caller

whose cold hands show a blueprint for next-world navigation,

hand-painted in sigils for the initiate's eyes only.

Left on Earth

Then, there was a moment that turned into more:

where the winds taste new, the way vacations

send the savor of a place without ties.

Had enough floes of sorrow from the arctic sameness

melted to an inlet of passion, opening the line of sight

one more mile toward its occluded shore?

What did it mean to be back in love

with the spinning globe, the sound of trains,

the thunder, the hoar of soft moonlight,

the daily treks of dog people in the street?

All photos of "the deceased" go nestled

into a writing desk that sits unused,

as if you gracefully recede to layers of space-time

I can't keep knocking on. Your smile concentrates
there, and in time will submit to review and recall
when enough days have drained of anguish.

For now, left on earth, the dream of stars is over.
A live man reacquaints me to the blossoming ground—
someone you sanction by way of fluke coincidence,
someone who charged out of the ether, not a knight
but another hiker through his own losses until he was
caught looking for me, and I recognized the path
made for the way of lovers walking.

Then, we who had for so long held firm to the familiar
shed our used notions onto the glad earth willingly,
to sprout the next phase where grief is venerated,
a pilgrimage through strange sights and close calls,
a body of work that topples the tower of safety.
He showed me how loss needn't inure as heaviness,
but can carry recollections of the beauty and the best of times.

Until you see that anyone can be felled by

grief so great it annihilates control,

you won't lay down with another

human's head on your chest and sleep

in peace. Until grief glistens like an

ancient sea basin under an honest sun,

you cannot land on level terrain dotted with

kindred and at last smile into the eyes that

welcome you to your next new home.

So, fortune gave me an untried key:

when I answered the dare to take

another's hand into my own,

release my wedding band

to the beautifully black river bottom soil,

and read the book in a stranger's face

only to find in it a tale much like my own.

PART III: Post-Season

The Bereaved Dead

Rain that shows itself as snow,

or snow obedient to the cadence

of rain? Can it be both?

Can a widow, sliced from her beloved

—approval fountain and limit maker—

know a merge with the All

so thoroughly she will never feel

tether again? No longer a choice—

both of them hope—

only the mystic widow dancing

inside the hut of single-point mind,

her steps polishing memories

until they gleam,

gamboling down a maze

of truths exhumed, those lost alleys

where the gold is found.

In either place she learns:

the one thing we own are our lives.

The dead suffer for us

as seasons deepen into cold, into white,

into stillness. They live in the rain

not quite ready for snow,

the brilliant leaves fallen, the gardens

gone to bed. Their going yet staying

is a gift we can't open.

And when skies pose a riddle,

we can cease the contortion

of our moments into narrative,

and deign to fall into Here,

the most sacred setting for Now.

The Song Cycles Around

Two years past the hospital

with its butterfly emblem

on your door signifying that

you were in flight to after-life,

I listen to every song I once

pretended was written for me.

I now hear differently

and from this distance,

appreciate a state of soul

so laid to waste that all I could do

was click into the night on every

Leonard Cohen dirge about love.

Hallelujah. I came back to life.

But every day Death shadows the breath

while in some moments I remember

that being left on Earth is to inhale

but a short time—a glittering time—

a mystery as grand as the transition

to stardust I'll make when your face

appears at the end of the tunnel.

Two years ago, that three a.m. in hospice

with its grueling details and strange

assurances left me certain that you

headed to authentic strata, neither inert

nor blank. But labels are tricksters—

speaking of realms, worlds, or planes?

Layers of being? Quantum consciousness?

Since I stood at the edge and stared in,

uncomprehending, I can't forget how

its otherness twines

our daily rounds of job and tribe.

Stubbornly, I roll with the blur

of daylight doings and worried nights,

nerves lit to influence the skin's bleak plain,

mind hitched to a constancy of debts

and to-do lists, the calendar's fits and starts,

grief ordered to dispel on time:

one year for spousal loss at most.

Most of us barely part the murk

of history and humiliations

in front of us, scrabbling for place among

those who manipulate appearances

to bypass their suffering and

intensify yours. Run, maze-rat, run.

But what if grief didn't have to

be carried out with the trash?

Some say it bursts gratuitously

into the arc of remembrance,

dropping hints for an expansion of heart

so sweeping as to rival the loss itself.

Why not give ourselves

to grief when grief comes asking?

Look into reports on what's next,

indulge hopes of a place beating with

the verities of love beyond love,

a library of ah-ha's stacked into

the silver linings:

a place you lost when falling into

a body, signing up for another stint

in the school of flesh, blood-steeped

and bonestrong with soul stirrings from

latitudes that words fail to touch.

Yet Another Burst

I know grief as the owl

with its clear syllable

of presence in the night.

I know grief as winter's

plumes done in evergreen,

all that's left when

flowers sleep. Wind-chill

pulls at each drape I add

to my body to deny

the cold, placate the entry

of one more bad memory,

losses reprised as a day's

unexpected turn of events.

Welcome home, grief.

Shoulder an old friend.

Hold the hand of grief

long enough and it opens

coffers of knowledge

too rugged for peace.

Lay your ear to this woe

and it will break open

a *piñata* of shame-seeds

tossed like candy,

a difficult food you must

convert on your own.

Walk broken into what is

no savage country, no

desert or badlands

but rife with places you

can go to evade the fetish

of Keeping Busy—

if

you can lessen long enough

your bigness

and know grief.

Dearest sorrow, I drop my face

into stone, uncomfortably

numb, your rules adhered:

no smile grows here,

no eyes spark. I greet your

watchers at the threshold, who

escort me to my room. To rest.

To rest. To incubate a dream

that forgets the world, a stasis

where no poems rise to pick at

the edifice of pain, and curtains

are drawn across darkness

to encourage the chrysalis,

a vulnerable way station that

may or may not release

the winged to fly.

I Can Tell

I can tell

by the way night's dreams

of you swell

I'm still holding onto you.

You were the harbor

where I belonged even when

storms drowned out the song.

Thanks for the rescue last night,

saying "Do it!"

when I languished in doubt.

We took our child too,

cooked our eggs, then flew

knowing together that any road will do—

I was holding onto you.

But no clothes of yours sequester
in closets here anymore.
No longer in dreams do you rise
from the loam, shedding your coffin
to walk the streets, drawing stares,
to knock bravely dirt-crumbed
on our front door.

I wake like a slab of trust gone bad.
Must I cling to a guide inside a man
who tells me when can't and when can?
So, never a choice is fully mine—
the bane of holding onto you?
Or is it that loving—for those who left—
constitutes their heaven, the Pure Land,
Valhalla? Or simply rest?

The truth is, since you died
and drought replaced the rains

of rumination I cried,

I still default to the spousal tie—

holding onto you,

wondering if you reach back, too.

Grief-Light for the Earth

I thought I could wait all night
for the moon. Fists around
white flowers with dark centers,
an offering to mown fields and
the lunar light on its way.

I hosted my demons with their
pointedly personal gripes:
hearing them out, feeling for
the ally-potential in them, now
and then scanning tree line
for the full Buck Moon. Blue.
Bigger. Brighter.

Plunked myself on the ground

too far south? This rare event

is taking its time. Better haul

sore knees to a more fitting perch—

but look, strands and swaths

of field gone ghostly. Had I only

turned around! Luna laughing,

throwing shine behind my back.

Following light, I see how she

leans in, the way a mother's face

breaks orbit when the chips

are so far down that someone's

wholly broken into jagged parts.

It's us, dear Lady, down here

firing at each other on our streets,

in schools, churches, grocery stores.

screaming bodiless through

keyboards of hate. And the oceans,

creatures, the enveloping air?

Smudged with lethal glop and ooze,

shapeless shrift that stops to stay.

Beneath moonglow's embrace,

cut prairie is sturdy in its resistance

to my shoes while working people

shutter and prepare for bed.

I don't know if it's privilege, luck, or

reckless abandon to be out now

on this supermoon shining night

beneath the oracle climbing

to see more of us—human strangers

struck silent, grieving distant nights

when earnest clans gathered

to gaze, confer, sip, and feast.

Remedy

You can never outrun grief

but beauty is a constant friend

that offers itself from daybreak

to nightfall, despite the hours

between when silence pulls time

away from rhythm and sense.

The woods green from below,

bright tags of brush that ignite

our bones to break free

into spring's penchant for

hope, renewal of plans,

and the naming of flowers.

And trees.

Oaks wait kindly to leaf,

letting others go first—

the redbuds who throw pixels

of purple at their knees and cry:

we stand for the eye! Whole

communities speak vivid color

to coax the sleeping trunks awake.

This, says beauty, is for you.

You can't leave grief behind

but the new sights of Spring

ascending beyond the door—

mornings even in metropolis

where the planted now bloom—

are not the only beauty

that shouts aloud to suffering.

Beauty of the beloved reveals

the vulnerable share,

beauty of the quiet talking

in tousled sheets and the clock

chiming duty as again,

there is that petition to the eye:

in the honest gaze, lover,

one is known.

Then they are gone,

by death or betrayal or disaster,

the bond ripped out by its roots

as happens in any season,

for grief knows them all.

Grief is not the sunderer who

made you go blind to beauty—

you did that when you steeled

yourself and said to let tears

be the past's portion, a finite

swallow purported to kill.

You thought you tricked it,

that leveler who wields

only loss and smashes normal.

Then grief returned with

its bowl begging for alms,

for it cannot help but see you.

Go, then, with senses tuned

to beauty, indulge at the feast

of color and warmth returning,

partner with the bud of unknown

origin and mysterious promise,

hear the faint hosannas of new

relationships that await or

will grow from change.

Catch the way beauty joins in

when grief walks among us,

for these two share the work

of force-flung creation

and dead-certain demise,

wordless but elegant with

their expressive immortal faces

that do not lie to you.

About the Author

Sue Westwind lives and writes in America's heartland, where she has the good fortune to live among woods that outline water. She is also the author of *Lunacy Lost: A Memoir of Green Mental Health* and, most recently, *The Land Erotic: A Memoir of Acres, Ecstasy & Marriage in Midlife & Beyond*, also published by Say Yes Quickly Books.

www.suewestwind.com

www.ingramcontent.com/pod-product-compliance
Lightning Source LLC
Chambersburg PA
CBHW070856050426
42453CB00012B/2239